This is Mr Chan's shop.

Mr Chan sells pens, pads and maps.

Tim is in Mr Chan's shop.

This is Miss Thin's shop.

Miss Thin sells eggs, nuts and carrots.

Tim is in Miss Thin's shop.

This is Mrs Ship's shop.

Mrs Ship sells jugs, shells and chess sets.

Tim is in Mrs Ship's shop.

This is Tim's rabbit!